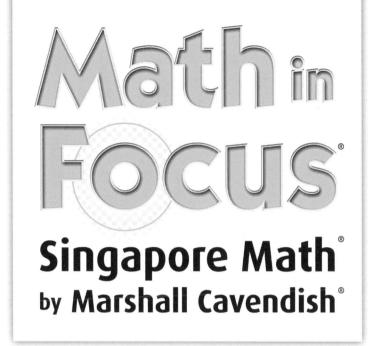

Math in Focus®

Singapore Math®
by Marshall Cavendish®

GRADE

KA

MW01001869

Student Book
Part 2

Author
Dr. Pamela Sharpe

U.S. Consultants
Andy Clark
Patsy F. Kanter

Marshall Cavendish
Education

U.S. Distributor

Houghton
Mifflin
Harcourt

© 2018 Marshall Cavendish Education Pte Ltd

Published by Marshall Cavendish Education
Times Centre, 1 New Industrial Road, Singapore 536196
Customer Service Hotline: (65) 6213 9688
US Office Tel: (1-914) 332 8888 | Fax: (1-914) 332 8882
E-mail: cs@mceducation.com
Website: www.mceducation.com

Distributed by
Houghton Mifflin Harcourt
222 Berkeley Street
Boston, MA 02116
Tel: 617-351-5000
Website: www.hmheducation.com/mathinfocus

Cover: © Bob Elsdale/Eureka/Alamy.
Image provided by Houghton Mifflin Harcourt.

First published 2018

ISBN 978-1-328-88058-1

Printed in Singapore

7 8 9 10   1401   24 23 22 21 20
4500814554   A B C D E

Contents

3 Order by Size, Length, or Weight

Lesson 1 Ordering Things by Size

Look and talk.

Which is the biggest? Color.
Which is the smallest? Circle.

Lesson 2 Comparing Sizes

Draw.

is **bigger than**

is **smaller than**

Draw.

is **taller than**

is **shorter than**

Color the longest snake yellow.
Color the shortest snake red.

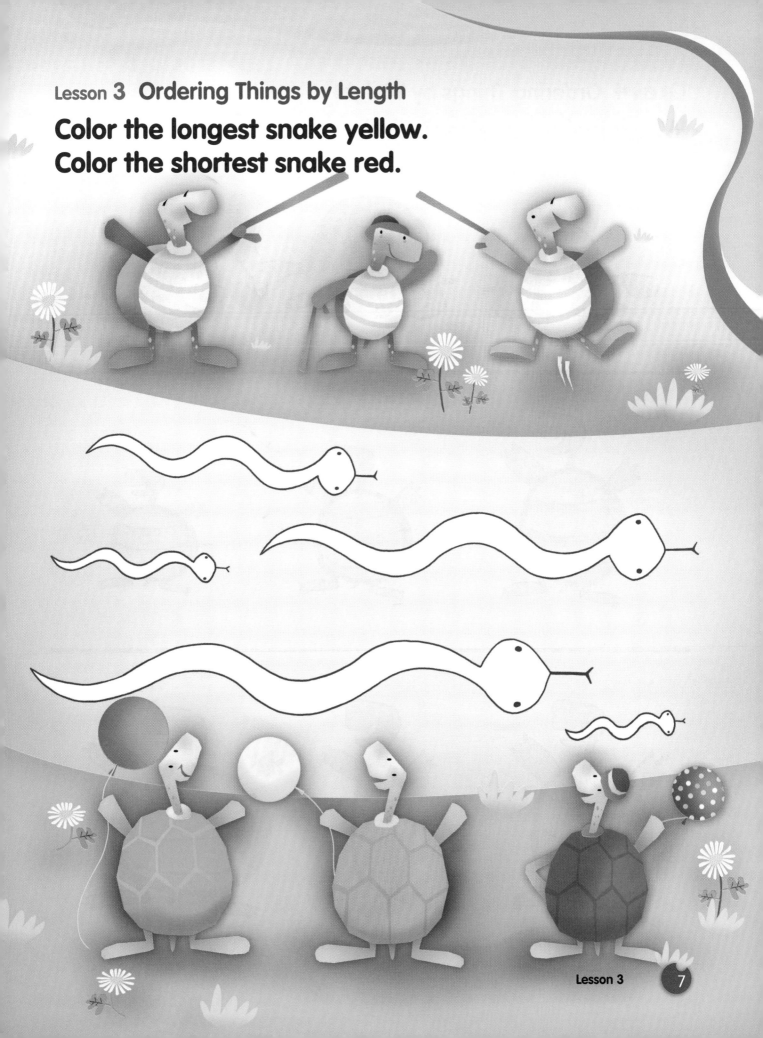

Which is the heaviest? Circle.

Chapter 4 Counting and Numbers 0 to 10

Lesson 1 Composing and Decomposing 5

Count, write, and circle.

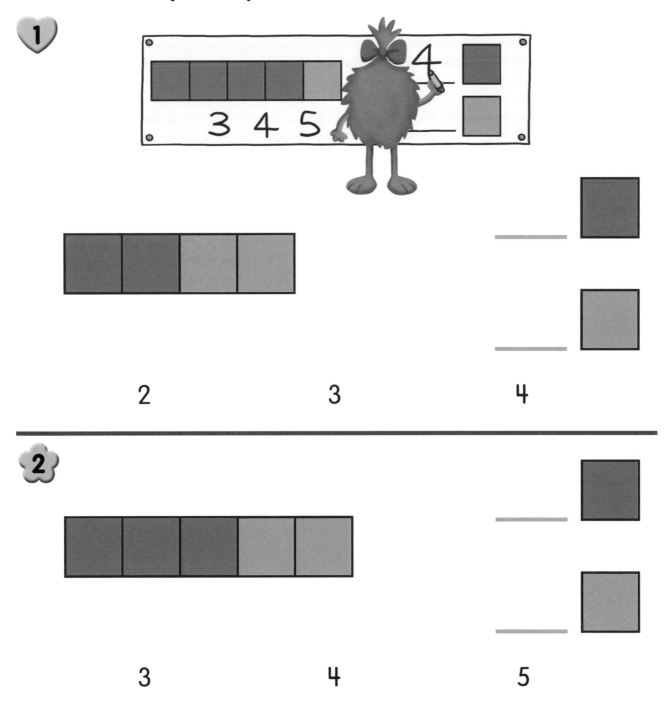

1

2   3   4

2

3   4   5

Color, count, and write.

 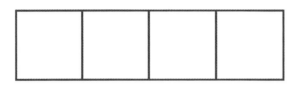

  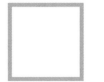

4 is _____ and _____.

 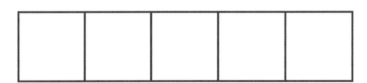

5 is _____ and _____.

5 is _____ and _____.

Are there enough? Color.

Draw enough .
Count and write.

_____   _____

Count and write.

Draw one more. Count and write.

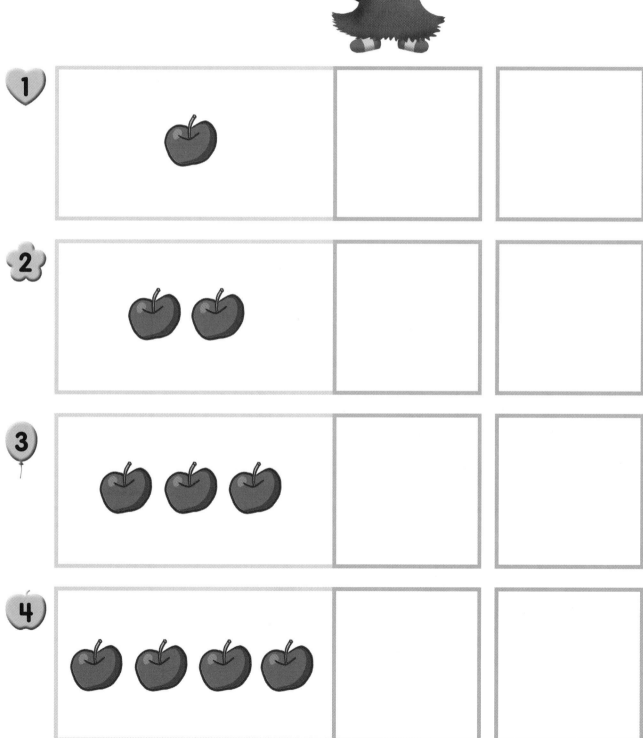

Count and write.

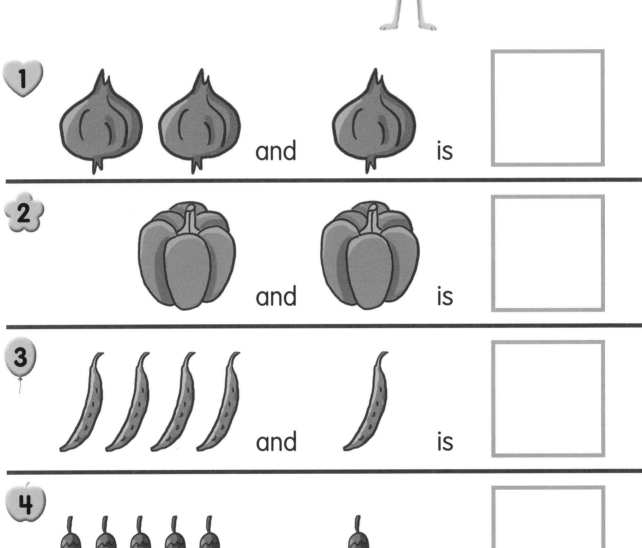

1. and is

2. and is

3. and is

4. and is

Draw, count, and write.

1

2

3

Lesson 3 Using Your Fingers and Toes to Count On
Count and write.

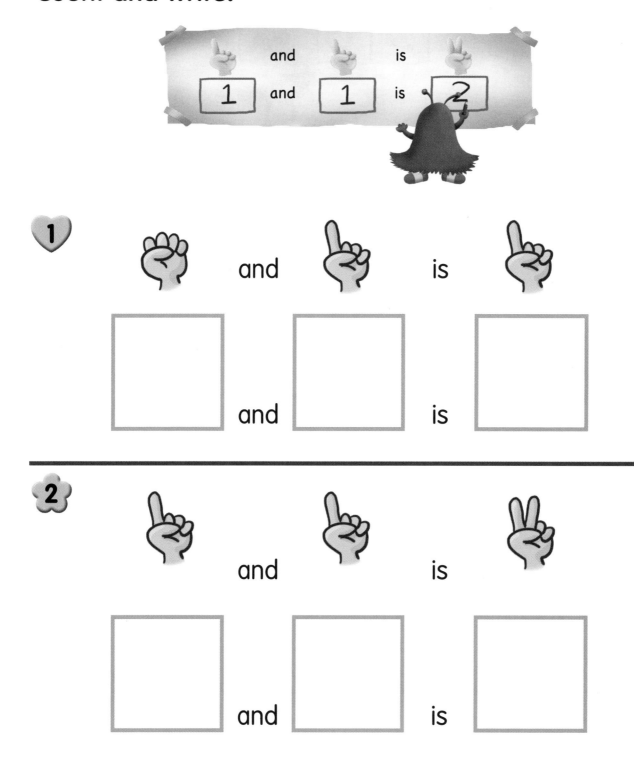

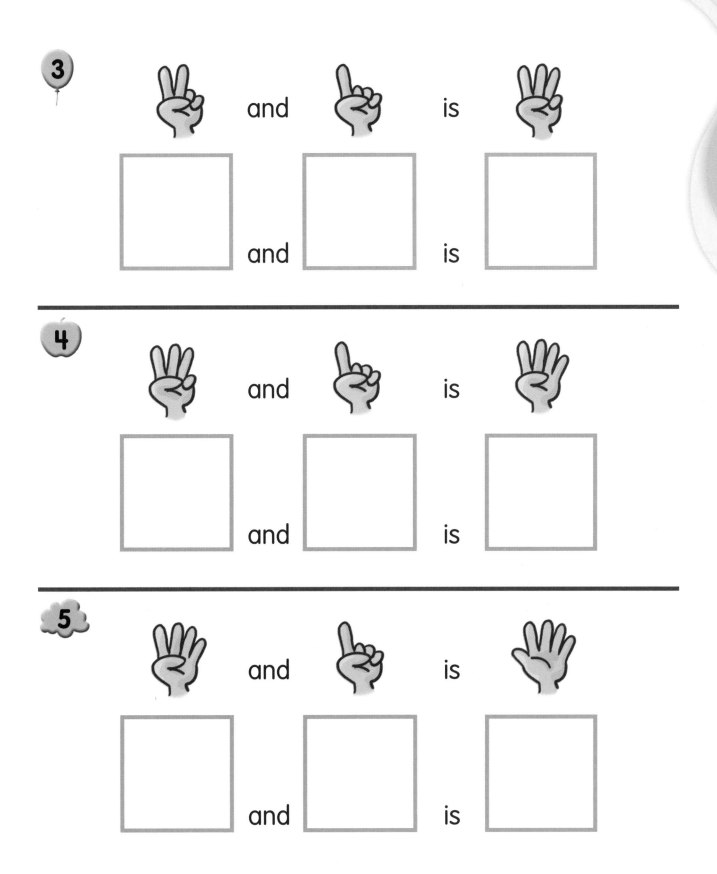

Look and talk.

How many more? Count and write.

Count and write.

1

_____ more flowers are needed.

2

_____ more flowers are needed.

3

_____ more flowers are needed.

Circle.

Which group has fewer than 3?

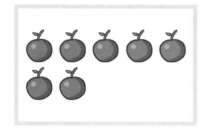  

Which group has fewer than 5?

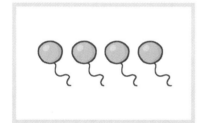 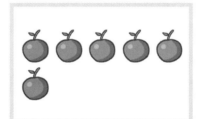 

Which group has fewer than 7?

  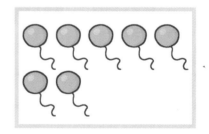

Which group has fewer than 9?

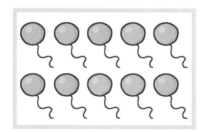  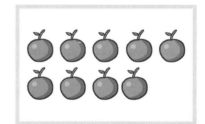

Draw one more. How many are there in all?

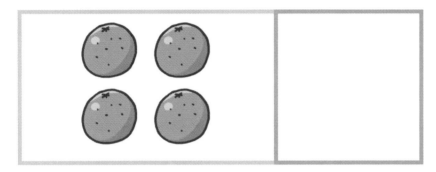

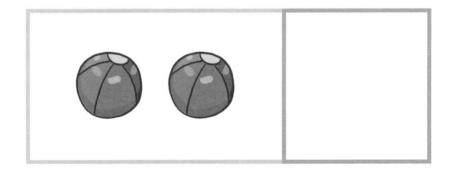

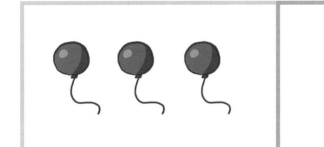

Circle, count, and write.

1 Vicki eats 2 grapes. Circle the grapes that are left behind.

_____ grapes are left behind.

---

2 2 birds fly away. Circle the birds that stay behind.

_____ birds stay behind.

---

3 4 horses trot away. Circle the horses that stay behind.

_____ horses stay behind.

Lesson 1   Big and Small Things

Draw.

Count and write.

Which will fit? Color.

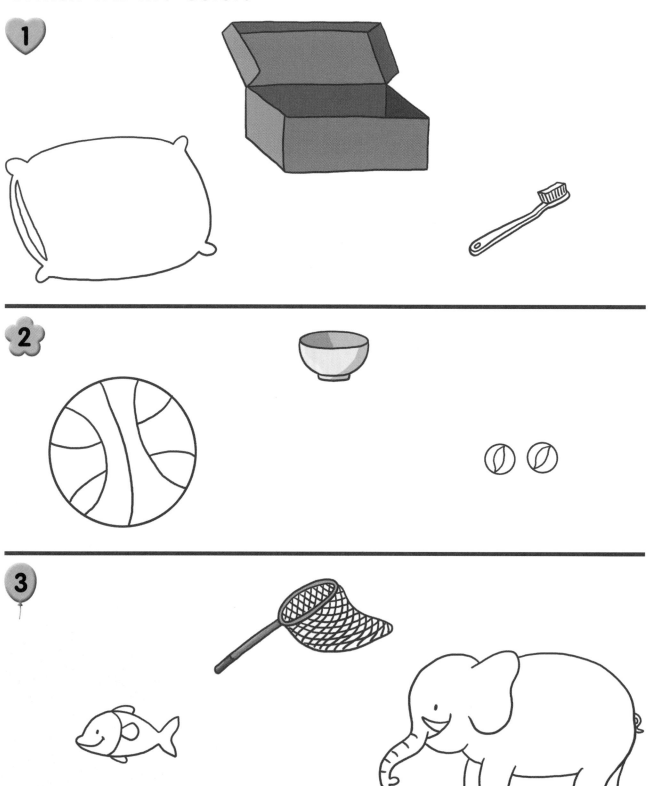

Pair.

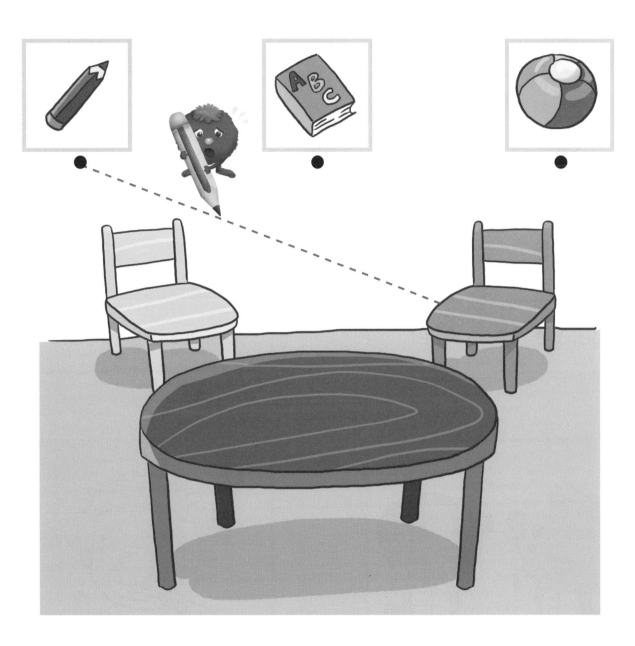

Color the box.

Before	After

Before	After

Before	After

Before	After

What do you do before school? Color.

What do you do after school? Color.

Lesson 1 All About 10

Sing.

One, two, buckle my shoe

Three, four, knock the door

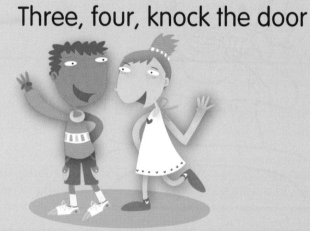

Five, six, pick up sticks

Seven, eight, lay them straight

Nine, ten, a big fat hen

Eleven, twelve,
Dig and delve

Thirteen, fourteen,
Maids a-sorting

Fifteen, sixteen,
Maids in the kitchen

Seventeen, eighteen,
Maids a-waiting

Nineteen, twenty,
My plate's empty!

Count and write.

2

Count and write.

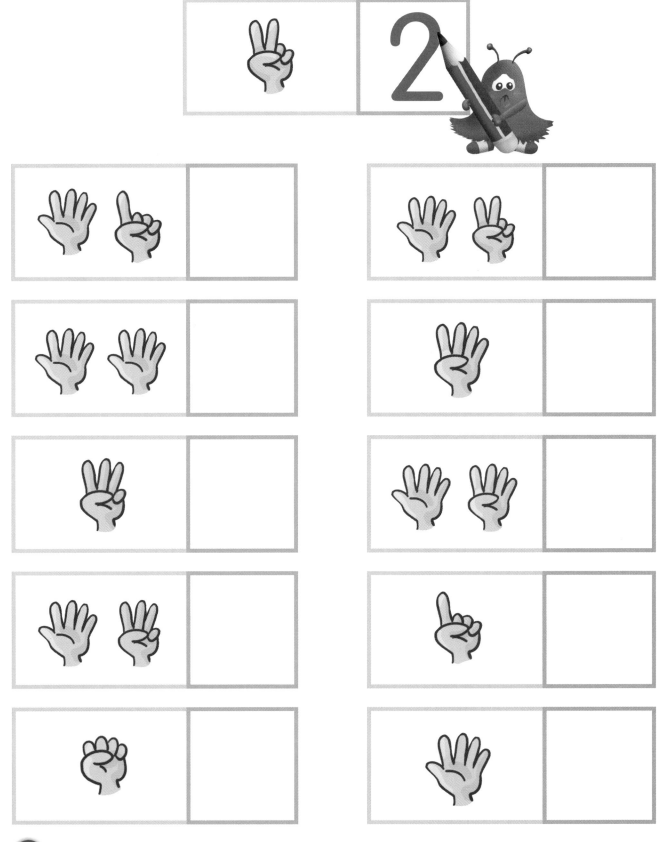

Count and write.

1 ♥

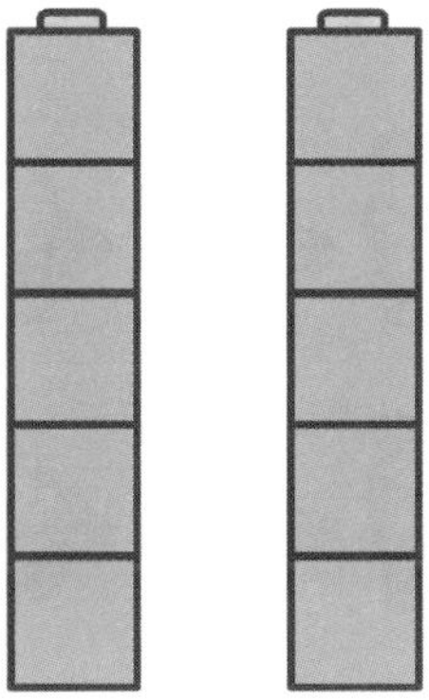

2 ✿

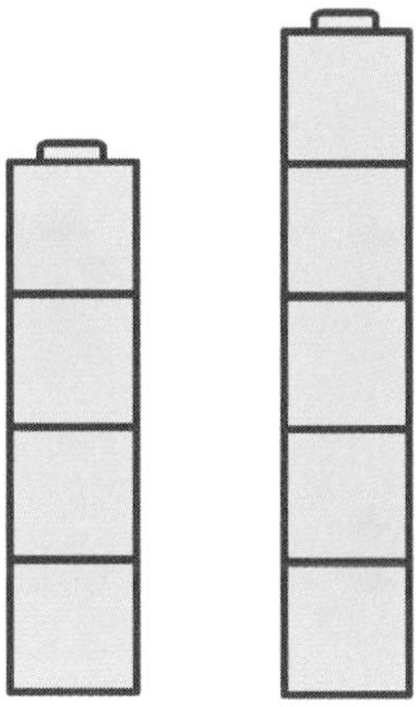

3 🎈

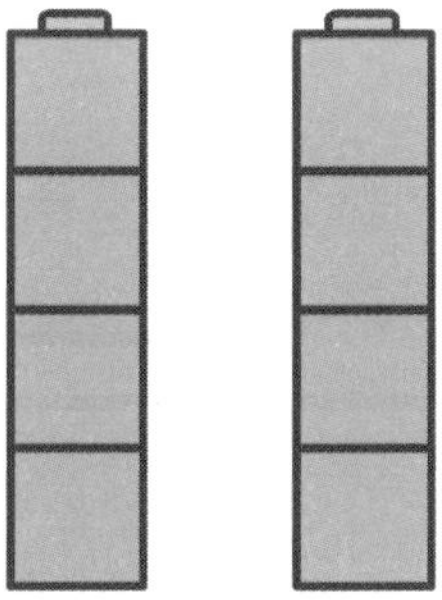

4 🍎

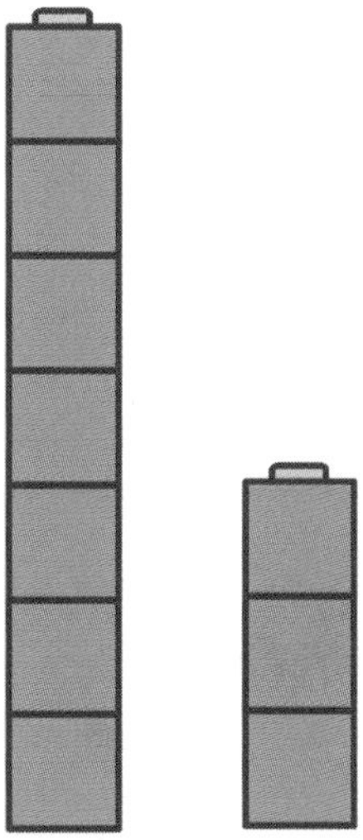

5 ☁

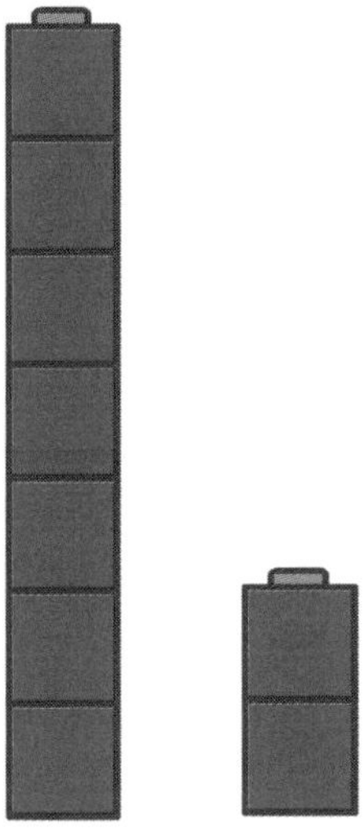

6 🍃

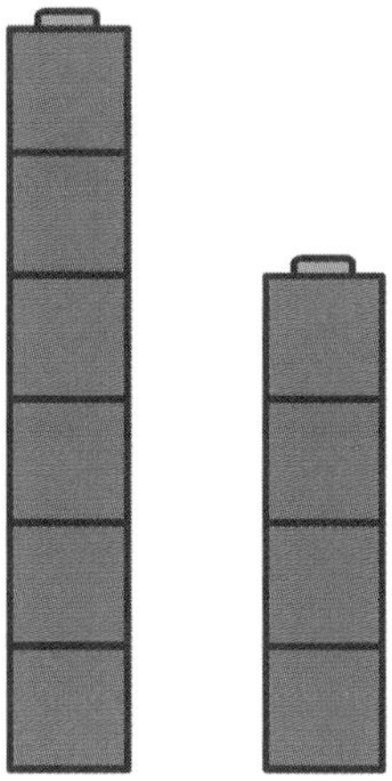

Count and write.

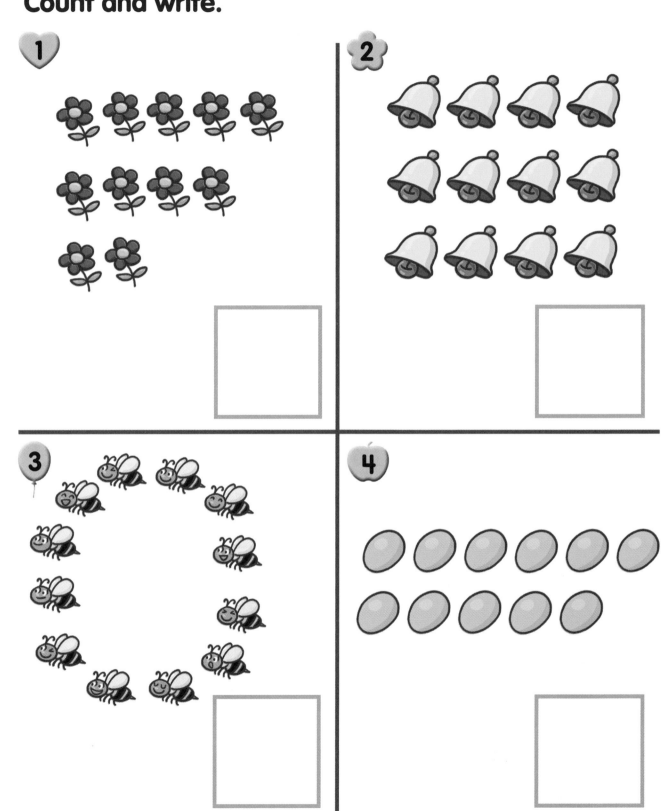

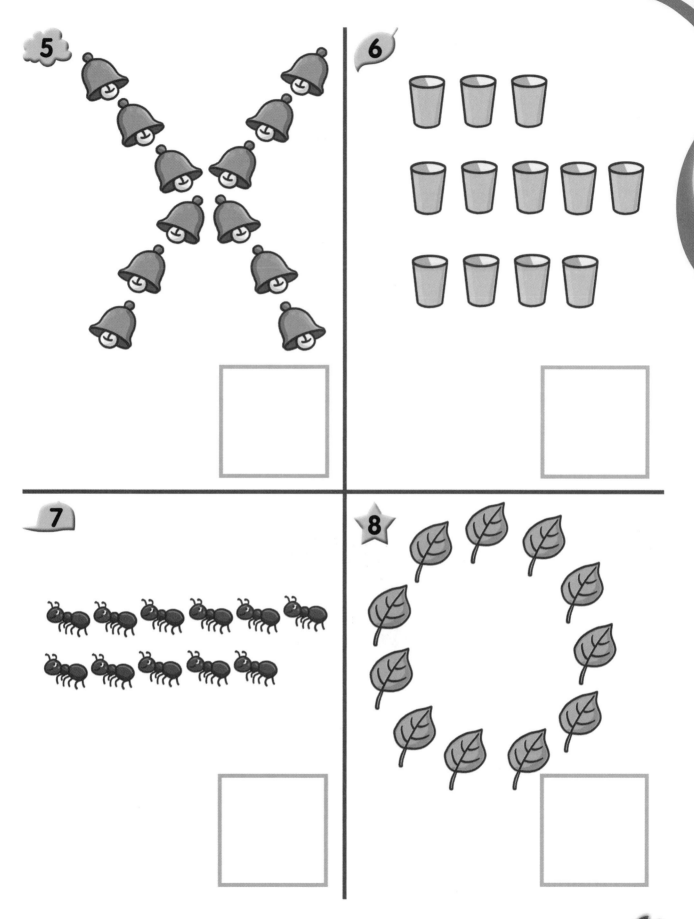

Read and draw ●. Count and write.

1

How many in all? _____

2

How many in all? _____

3

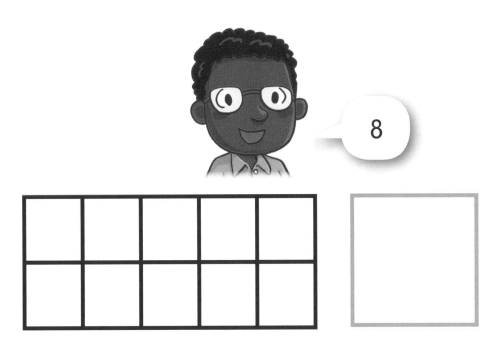

How many in all? _____

4

How many in all? _____

Count and write.

4

⭐⭐⭐⭐⭐ ⭐⭐⭐⭐
⭐⭐⭐⭐⭐

5

6

Count and write.

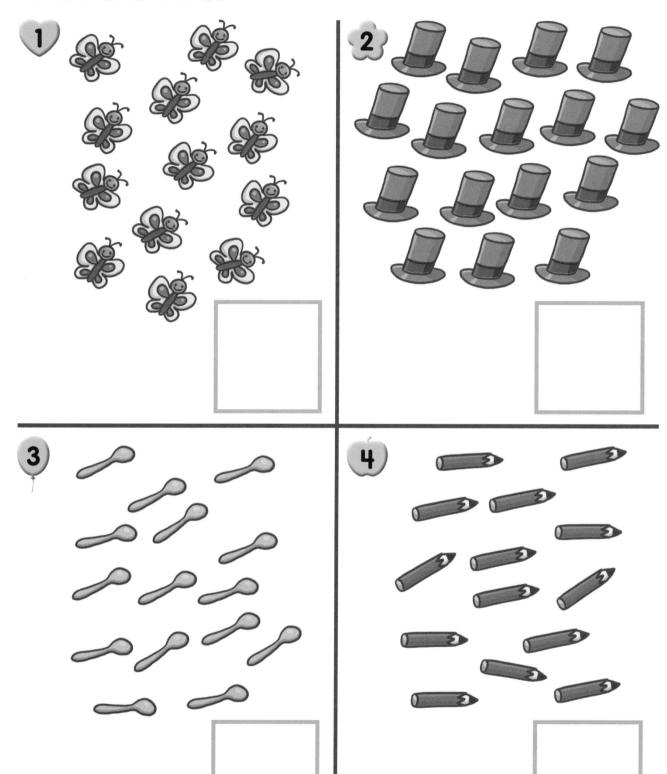

Count and write.

 1

 2

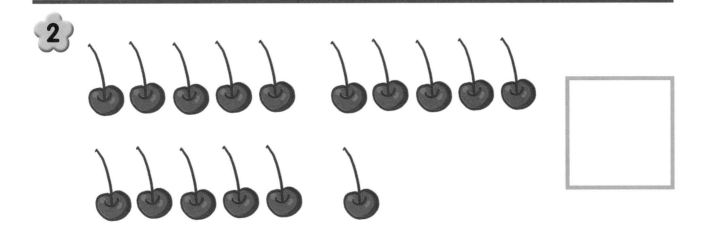

3

Count and write.

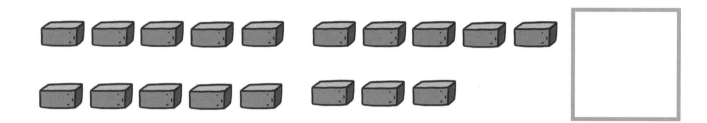

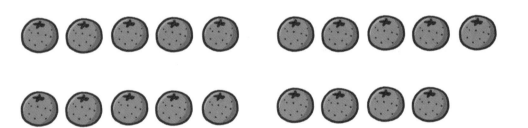

Count and write.

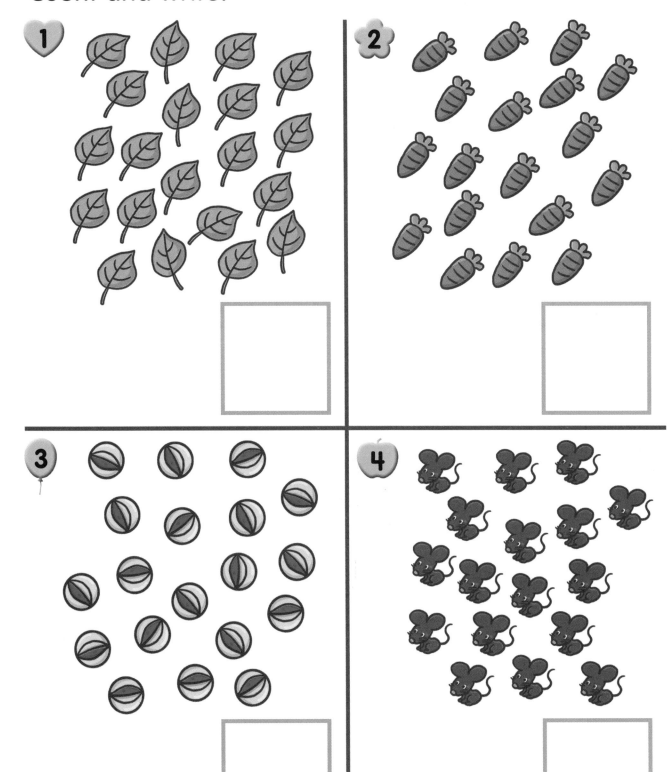

1

2

3

4

Read and draw . Count and write.

1

18

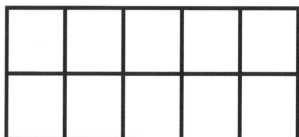

How many in all? _____

2

16

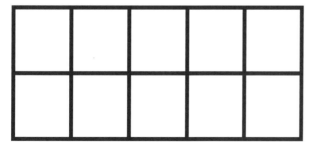 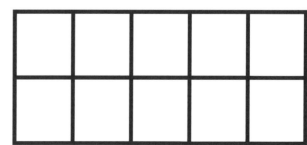

How many in all? _____

3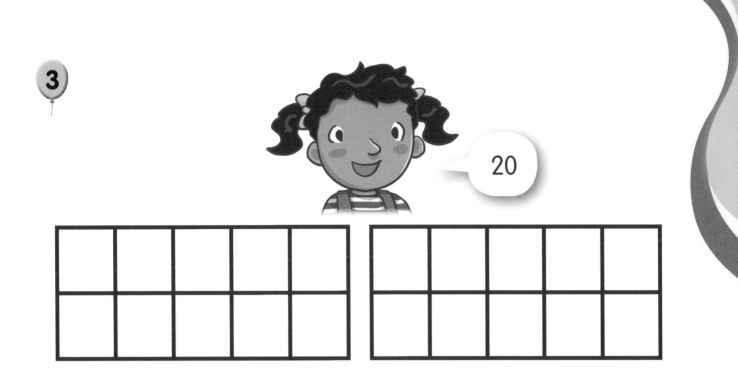

How many in all? _____

4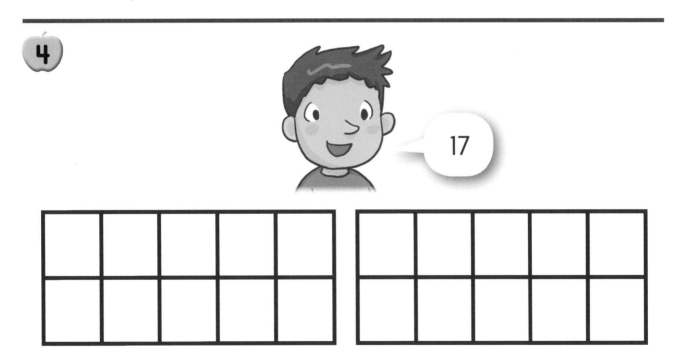

How many in all? _____

Read and draw . Count and write.

How many in all? _____

How many in all? _____

Join the dots.

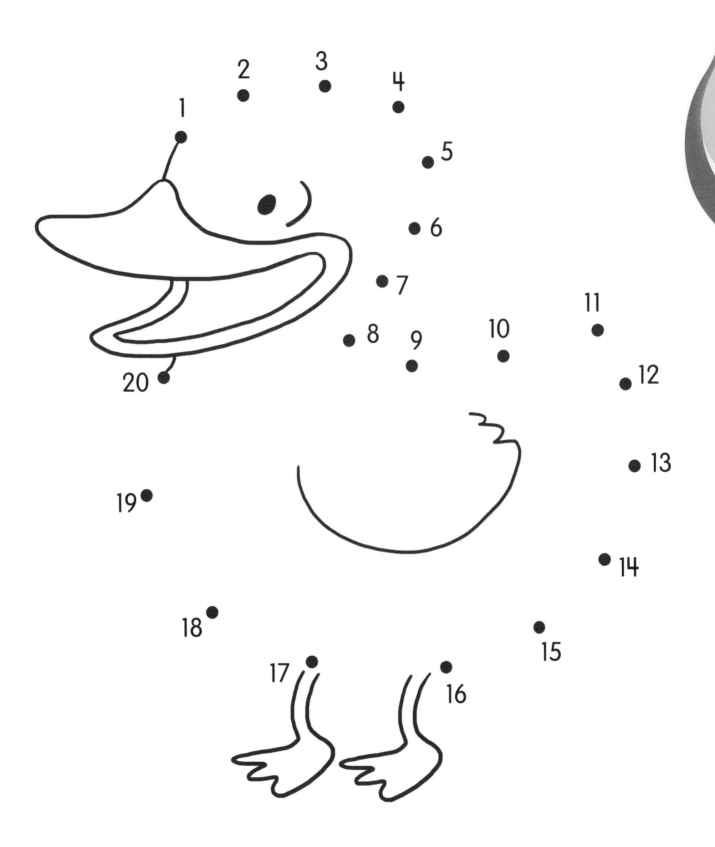

Count and write. Color the group with more.

_____ ☆   _____ ♡

Count and write. Color the group with fewer.

_____    _____

Draw the same number.

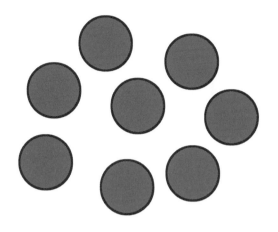

Draw more.

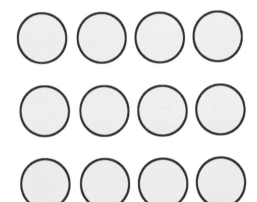

Draw fewer.

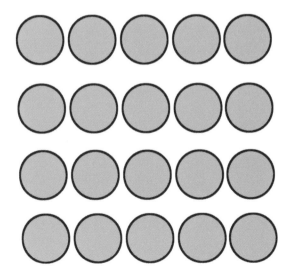

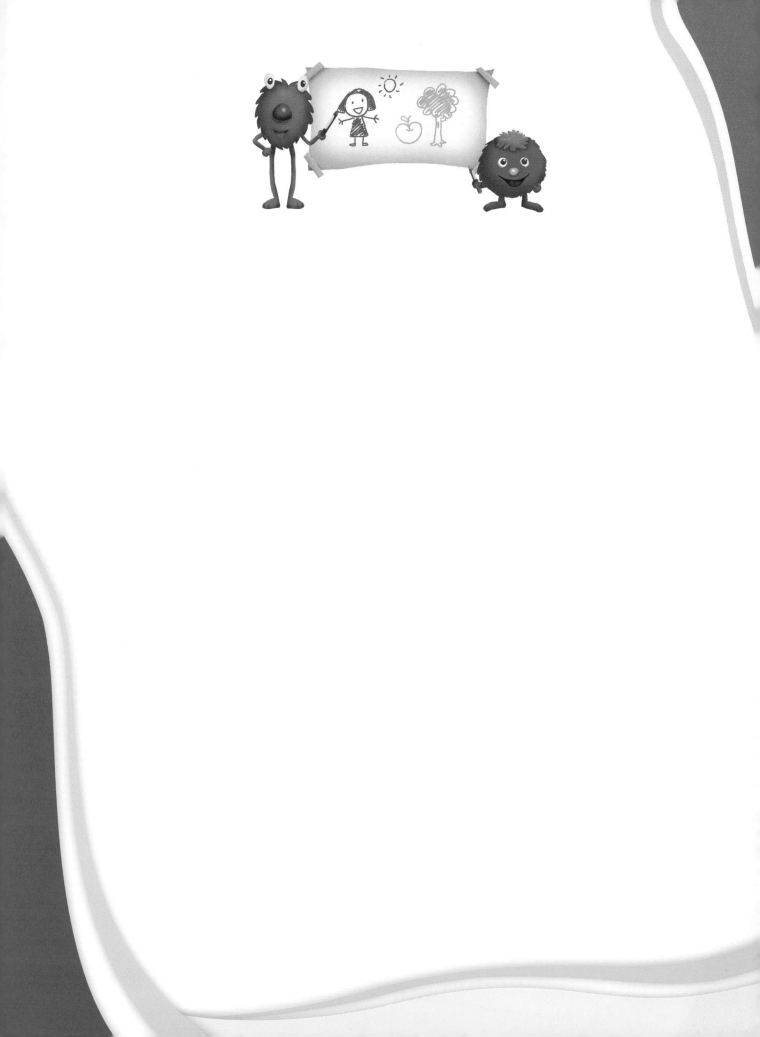